Tonguit

Tonguit

Harry Giles

FREIGHT BOOKS

First published 2015
By Freight Books
49-53 Virginia Street
Glasgow, G1 1TS
www.freightbooks.co.uk

A CIP catalogue reference for this book is available from the British Library.

ISBN 978-1-910449-36-3

Typeset by Freight in Meta Serif
Printed and bound by Bell and Bain, Glasgow

the publisher acknowledges investment from
Creative Scotland toward the publication of this book

Contents

Acknowledgements

Previous versions of some of these poems have appeared in *Pank*, *Magma*, *Poems in Which*, *Blind Poetics*, *Fit to Work*, *Clinic*, *New Writing Scotland*, *The List*, *Inspired by Independence*, *Scotia Nova*, *the National Collective Zine*, *Valve*, *Naked Among Thistles*, *The Rag*, *A Bird Is Not A Stone*, *Tour de Vers*, *Be the First to Like This*, *Gutter*, *In Protest*, and in the pamphlets *Visa Wedding* and *Oam* from Stewed Rhubarb Press. *If you measure the distance...* won the IdeasTap Poetry Competition 2012. The poems of Govanhill Baths were written on residency there in 2013.

Brave

Acause incomer will aywis be a clarty wird,
acause this tongue A gabber wi will nivver be the real
  Mackay, A sing.
Acause fer aw that we're aw Jock Tamson's etcetera, are we
  tho? Eh? Are we.
Acause o muntains, castles, tenements n backlans,
acause o whisky exports, acause o airports,
acause o islans, A sing.
acause o pubs whit arena daein sae weel oot o the smokin
  ban, A sing.
acause hit's grand tae sit wi a lexicon n a deeskit mynd, A
  sing.
acause o the pish in the stair, A sing.
acause o ye,

A sing o a Scotland whit wadna ken workin class
  authenticity gin hit cam reelin aff an ile rig douned six
  pints o Tennent's n glasst hit in the cunt,
            whit hit wadna
                  by the way.

A sing o google Scotland,
            o laptop Scotland,
                  o a Scotland sae dowf on bit-torrentit HBO
                  drama series n DLC packs fer
                  paistapocalyptic RPGs that hit wadna ken
                  hits gowk fae hits gadjie,
                        tae whas lips n fingers amazebawz cams
                        mair freely as bangin.

A sing o a Scotland whit hinks the preservation o an
  evendoun Scots leeteratur is o parteecular vailyie n
  importance bit cadna write hit wi a reproduction claymore
  shairp on hits craig,
            whit hinks Walter Scott scrievit in an either tide,
            whit hinks Irvine Welsh scrievit in an either tide.

A sing o a Scotland whit wants independence fae Tories
n patronisin keeks
n chips on shoulders
bit sprattles tae assert ony kin o
cultural autonomy whit isna
grundit in honeytraps.

A sing o a Scotland whit hinks thare's likely some sort o
God, richt?
whit wad like tae gang fer sushi wan nicht but cadna
haundle chopsticks,
whit signs up fur internet datin profiles n nivver
replies tae the messages,
whit dreams o bidin in London.

A sing o a Scotland whit fires tourists weirin See You Jimmy
hats the puir deathstare,
n made a pynt o learnin aw the varses tae Auld
Lang Syne,
n awns a hail signed collection o Belle n
Sebastian EPs.

A sing o a Scotland bidin in real dreid o wan day findin oot
juist hou parochial aw hits cultural references mey be,
n cin only cope wi the intertextuality o the Scots
Renaissance wi whappin annotatit editions,
n weens hits the same wi awbdy else.

A sing o a Scotland whit hasna gied tae Skye,
or Scrabster,
or Scone,
bit cin do ye an absolute dymont o
a rant on the plurality o Scots
identity fae Alexandair mac
Alexandair tae Wee Eck.

A sing o a Scotland whit cadna hink o a grander wey tae
end a nicht as wi a poke o chips n curry sauce,
>   whit chacks the date o Bannockburn on
>   Wikipaedia,
>   whit's no sae shuir aboot proportional
>   representation,
>   whit draws chairts on the backs o beermats tae
>   learn ye aboot rifts n glaciation
>>   n when hit dis hit feels this oorie dunk,
>>   this undesairvt wairmth
>>   o inexplicable luve,
>   whit is heavt up,
>>   in the blenks afore anxiety is heavt up
>>   by the lithe curve o a firth.
Whit wants ye tae catch the drift.
Whit's stairtin tae loss the pynt.

A sing o a Scotland whit'll chant hits hairt oot dounstairs
o the Royal Oak, whit'll pouk hits timmer clarsach
hairtstrangs, whit like glamour will sing hits hairt intae
existence, whit haps sang roon hits bluidy nieve hairt,

>   whit sings.

Instructions for Behaviour at Border Control

Wear a red dress. Paint your eyebrows green. Ensure
your gait mimics the gait of a lion who's fallen
awkwardly from the sofa and is pretending he hasn't.

Hop sideways and shifty across the line that reads PLEASE
STAND HERE. Throat lustily *Now you see me Now
you don't.* Fall to one knee with a ring made of fluorescent

plastic and zebra-skin. Ask the loneliest guard to marry you.
Stroke her gun. Whisper in earnest *I studied witchcraft*
then grin because with your green eyebrows she can't but
  know

you are telling a truth. While stamping out hours of queue,
ignoring the teeth of glossy instructional vids, invent
a Magnificent Teleportation Device, and with its tachyon
  trails

write theories of history to gut the future. Return, steaming,
and sing of this to the queue and the guards and the screens
  and the signs
till the thrice-damned terminal implodes from the singular
  weight

of its own internal contradictions. And breathe again. And spell
again the teleportation device, the manifesto, the implosion.
Make a lever of your time. Handle yourself with care.

Curriculum

Paint me an equation, lover, and paint it
in all the percussion of your tuneless tongue.
Brew me magic potions in the High School
laboratory. Hex the vaulting horse.

Mix me a metaphor of noble gases,
economic engines and avant-garde
taxonomies, with Kingdom Phylum Order
gone to bloody Dada. Get down and dirty

with transects, quadrants. Take the DSM
and shove it, shove it somewhere pretty, like
a lady sawn in half. Fuck the whole
syllabus, fuck sideways, stick a pin

in the course catalogue, then do it again
but do it harder. Do it slowly. Do it
till what you want burns blue, bright, black,
and hold till every reference is earth.

Visa Wedding

Listen, hit's semple:

in Orkney A'm English;
in England A'm Scottish;
in Scotland, Orcadian –

this glib-gabbit, mony-littit tongue
snacks at identity as tho hit wis
a gollach piece sappit wi
the sweet-n-soor o BELONG.

Like aw thay ither sangsters A

ballad the islans fae the ceety,
buzz the ceety fae the islans,
birn frantic throu hydrocarbons

fer transatlantic jouks whar hame
is happit in bacon, fried on grits,
tursit in that muckle myndin n mad-on
ancestry hit's at lang n lenth hausable.

Hey, haud me close, America,

mak me yer kiltie mascot,
mak me yer islan exotic,
mak me yer immigrant boy,

mowten me wi soothren sun n muntain
fir-sap n ser me on ice-cream,
unnest me, unnest me, shaw me vistas,
spreid me skinkin ower strath n hill-run.

Leuk, A growed-up dancin

the Gay Gordons tae Blanket on the Grund,
Strippit the Willow tae On the Bayou,
shauchled n spittit ilka wird o Hit the Road

Jack n nivver cam back nae mair, gie me
laund lots o laund, tak me hame tae the place
A belang, send me aff ferivver but
A ask ye please, no more nae mair no more.

Reception

A beam british agin yer
american orthodoxy, faimlie:
ye're hella glaise n thay greens
gust puir bangin tae a tannin tongue,
but A rackon A greet ironic, grin
creukit, mair weblike as gridplan.

Jings, n this vyce is fleetin aw
midatlantic, like, or hopscotchin
astride Hadrian's waw, hid hauf
in newins, hauf in camouflage.
But izzit tho? Ye want tae ken
ma origin story. Hit's no spelt

in ionic columns n firs as wis
yer dear dear revolution, kin,
n hit michtna be telt at aw.
Tho but, A'm smuiricht yer grans
n trees nou, n see ma scrans
o forest wi a fremmit ee.

Honeymoon

At the edge o a time, the tide n the licht begin
tae tell thair sweir-drawn bye-the-nou thegither –
the saft saund-slaikin-straikin, the sunslant
stellin an oor in lammer, the ootrug gaun
a bittie faurder ilka turn – awthegither:

> twa walcome guests wae tae awa, mindin on
> tae speir at yer bairns, n syne, a wheen
> stappies nearer the door, turnin tae say
> *hoo leesom* n *wi maun* n *mair aft*,
> n sic n sic-like, till watcht doun the road.

Nou, in this ower-seendle times, the stanes,
weetit n luntit, warship. Thay are colour.
Saphir, ruby, dymont, dymont – ye wadna
hae trouit thare wis that mony jems i the warld,
that mony prisms on wan weel-kent strand.

Piercings

It took two looks to see him,
head whipped and jaw loosed, silent
moviewise. The boy who broke me in,
my nut, my skin, up, who said *a break-*
down would do you good. The change

snuck him past me, but: same flesh,
same stride. I called. We spoke.
The quick, smiling chat of two
folk who knew inside each other's
mouths, but not heads. I looked hard.

The difference wasn't clear, and then
it was. The lipring that turned
his pout sullen, hot. The jangle
of earrings I'd buried my face in
as he steel-tracked my heavy

shoulders. The scaffold. The sharp,
shocking stud in his busy tongue.
All gone. In the four years since
he hauled me into a lift with
Want to make out?, he'd pulled

out every metal sign, become
employable, less obvious. I'd paid
ten quid in Camden for my first, made
more holes each time I got depressed.
Got inked. He asked, *So what do you do now?*

Slash poem in which Harry Giles meets Harry Styles

Harry, are you going to
play hard to get? Harry,
what kind of boys do
you like? This stupid dance
isn't school. Harry, please keep

your kisses to yourself. Do
you want a drink before
we start? Harry, are you
OK? Harry, get your hands
off me. Harry, make me.

I want you to come
with me, Harry. I want
you to stretch your legs,
Harry, I want to get
on the floor, I want

to use teeth and tongue.
You're blushing, Harry. I don't
think your jokes are funny.
Harry, tell me what happened.
Why is it always me?

What was that, babe? Harry,
would you cry if I
stepped on your foot? Harry,
don't pretend you're not mine.
Harry, don't spoil this rhyme.

Waffle House Crush

I'll have you smothered n covered n
diced n peppered n
capped n lathered n
lustred n smoothed n
spread

drizzled n dazzled n
blazed n baked n
blended n buttered n
shined n sprinkled n
seared

creamed n candied n
steamed n whipped n
stuffed n sugared n
spiced n simmered n
oiled,

reduced,

heaped,

dressed,

n can I get some coffee with that?

Poem in which nouns, verbs and adjectives have been replaced by entries from the Wikipedia page *List of Fantasy Worlds*

You gor me. Boxen in your sartorias-deles
and angeous krynn. Too xanth, too zothique,
as though an erde of bas-lag were termina
under your hyrule. As though I were charn

already. Don't beklan to me, don't tir like
I'm lodoss to your emelan blest,
like I'll xen when you tortall my deverry tarth,
ooo, I'd landover earthsea with you, panem.

It's erehwon. You're still melniboné,
your eberron oz and aebrynis quin are still
spira. I nirn you. But faltha your athas
and then you can halla me. Og idris:

eidolon to pern me, tamriel! Harn me till
all my mundus aurbis one glorantha *Eä!*

Song for a Lover as Magicicada

you emerged   in tremendous   volumes   wee septendecim
   nymph   of Brood X   a serious   song
      already   cracking   from root-   sucking   lips
the drum and scream of prime   number   music

snap snap   across   the cottonwood   congregation
   to snap   my wings to your   *PHARAOH   PHARAOH-*
    OH-   *OH!* is worth   the prep   ostererous
      math emat ical   wait   your tymbals quaking

       PHARAOH ARMY SURE GOT DROWNDED
       PHARAOH PHARAOH OH OH OH PHARAOH
       SURE GOT DROWNDED GO DOWN GO
       DOWN AND GO DOWN AND AND DOWN AND

(and white noise   now keeps you   awake?   no wonder!
   my heart   you must hear   this brood-song in wires
  in walls   in traffic   through windows   through web
must hunt   the teeming world with your call and tease

                the unfeasible chorus

                for a single

                answering

                click)

If you measure the distance between the teeth they'll tell you

so it turns out the fossil of a cricket
        is a lossless audio codec
is a phonograph cylinder expecting the right
        mandrel and needle
hey Indestructible Record Company you know squat
        against the fossil record

        because the silt was so fine
even the undersides of the wings were preserved
        we could see the ridges of teeth
we cannot contain our glee / it is written all over the news
        that cricket, cricket
after one hundred sixty five million years your single chirrup
        loops from my laptop

        the cricket's song is deeper
than the crickets' of today / he boomed the Jurassic
        acoustic landscape
you can reconstruct behaviours / my boreal songs are filed
        in malleus, incus, stapes
are written in the function of my vast lungs

how terrifyingly airless the oceans would be
        without blue-green algae
my song stems from single-celled
        bloom / a song
of respiration / a song / a song / a vibration
        through populous strata
        through one thousand ninety three patents
        through dissected organs
and digital models / till now crickets sing beyond our hearing

Pantoum on Reading Wikipedia's
Timeline of the Far Future

First, the Niagara Falls, carving their way
back to their mother, will cease to exist. By then,
the brake of the moon will have slowed us a second a day.
No matter our carbon, the blanket ice will send

us back to our mother. We'll cease to exist. By then,
a supervolcano will surely have opened its arms,
no matter our carbon. The blanket ice will send
a white kiss to the sun. The earth cools, and warms.

A supervolcano will surely have opened its arms
before the surviving coral rebuilds, before
our white kiss to the sun. The earth cools, and warms,
and cools. A continent will open, and roar

before the surviving coral rebuilds, before
we lose all the old mountains. A meteor strikes,
and cools. A continent opens, and roars.
And, further out, a great moon's flight

will close. In the old mountains, his fall strikes.
We cannot see much further. Our numbers go dark
as, further out, the great rings' flight
reels into dust. Beyond this mark

we cannot see further. Our numbers go dark
due to the limitations of time, who
reels into dust. Beyond this mark
we only know the system turns, that you,

due to the limitations of time, due
to the brute physics, are a shaking echo.
We do know the system turns, that you,
in the moons' fall, the planets' crash, are owed

to the brute physics. Is a shaking echo
enough? Do you need to know yourself more
than the moons' fall? The planets' crash? You're owed
nothing by entropy, but you are given a store

enough for your needs. To know yourself more
is really nothing but luck, nothing but spin,
nothing but entropy. You are given a store
of half-held understanding, and here you begin:

there's really nothing but luck, nothing but spin.
The brake of the moon will slow us a second a day:
half-hold this understanding, and here you begin.
First, the Niagara Falls, carving their way.

Hidden Track

fast forward through the empty bits

as if trampling eggs   as if goading a perp

to admit it

as if keen as if scissors to trim

from a lexicon all the strings   you will not ever

use   as if the dead air

were not a test   as if you will never pass

into speechlessness   as if your heart will never rot

Maeshowe
Chambered Cairn, Winter Solstice

Lown i the lair
o five thoosan year,
we wauk the luntit
lip o winter
whiles hit sains
the runit flags.

We're suithless: gabbin,
lowsin shaidaes,
raxin fer some kin o
mynd i the muivement
o starns n stanes.

Haud haunds n braith.
Aw unconcernit
the thief cried sun
steals intae the rouk.

The wicht cried muin
taks back the lift.
Wi sou wi the birlin.

Banes wir nivver
kistit here.

Nae faith but in time.

Piazza dei Miracoli

36 humans are
posing to shore
up a world, but
8 more are here
to edge us over.

And if not them, then
who will save us? Then
what burnt and ropey
limbs will brace our
breath? Brave smiles!
Marble glow, grubby,
toothsome glow, all
delectable, cock-eyed,
hilarious perspective.
What camera smiles!
Spangled on bollards
and desperate lawns,
holding up for home.

Sweat patch: miracle!
Cargo shorts: miracle!
Arkansas, handshake,
manbag, rough guide,
yes: miracle, miracle.

Dear soured day-trip
economy, mourn not,
for your red and gold
houses of learning are
now written over with
the zigzag slogans and
arrows of your own
long enduring miracle!
But, despite the best of illusions,
a century later they will make terrible jokes of the ruins.

Govanhill Baths, July 2013

steel shutters / brusts
fae reid brick a bluimin
purpie horn

*

pent pirls awa
i the heat / rannoch sclims
roustin rone-pipes

*

thunner-plump ower-
flowes the ruif / fog unmortarin
wir hie reid waw

*

airn wreath, gowd pent /
forhooiet wab catches time
fae the doun-heid-clock

*

a puil's dry lenths /
i the deep end, unseasonal
algal bluim

*

boots on auld
white tiles / somethin saft gies wey,
some wee herb

Nicht Shift at the Slipper Baths

Sheu scrapes aff her uniform, tirds hersel,
hings the nicht on a wee metal cleek,
douks her fit in the watter n skirls
tae the gliff o heat – skirls n scriechs,

fer aye that bath's like a kiss aw ower –
rives knees up tae oxters n screenges awa
wi a wee bit carbolic (wan baur atween fower).
Cath batters her waw sae sheu flips the smaw

      scran o saip. Hits airc dreeps couth.
      Cath yaffs as hit cloots her richt i the mooth.

That wifie wi the purse fair scowls,
n wheeshts thaim like thay're in kirk bare-airsed.
Thay turn thair pusses up n yowl
n the sun stairts trinklin throu the gless.

Blue Ghaists

Blue ghaists aye swith up n doun the puil.
Twa hunner tuithie ghaists cheer fae the balconies,
    clap ghaist haunds,
n a skinklin ghaist swees fae the ghaist trapeze
    ower the ghaist watter.

Ween ye soond here, the sang ye're gien
isna an echa but the answerin yowt
    o a ghaist diver
at lang n lenth makkin her threeple somersault
    abuin the ghaist watter.

The ghaist-snoker said thare are guideens n badeens.
Yer finger-thrum's a wean sayin *Come in,*
    play Murderball,
n the grue up your thees is the gless ee turnin
    unner the ghaist watter.

Gin we droun the stage in wallie sweemable
watter, gin we dicht the waws n scrape
    aff the ghaist grandur,
n appen doors tae bid the ghaists escape
    ootae the ghaist watter,

n fill the puil wi galas, pairties, lenths –
A hink the best is, that mony o the last
    century's speerits
wad walcome ninety mair years o ghaists
    intae the watter.

Hoo tae Chap an Ingan

Appen wan end n huil
     the teuchest layers,
   twa-three anely.

          Coll it
             then haud
                   the guid big hairt.

     Hauf hit wi a trig cut.

Set the pairts plat
   n begin wi
               tentie slices
– nae need fer prossin
        speedy haunds.

          Be cannie, keepin
        the root atween
               thoumb n courag.

        Haud hit thegither
             n cut the ither wey.

Aye, ye'll greet –
    hit's juist fer the ingan
        's that guid.

Wash yer haunds in cauld watter.

             Soon ye'll hae
        a hunner guid
      bitties o ingan.

    The last pairt is
          drap thaim in a pot
whit's tae be shairt.

In yer haunds thare are nae deid hings

A haurd ye lairn the healin airts
tae the yaupie: thare's nae auld dud
gaes ithoot a shot at bein
happit roon a hairt again.
Whit's rubbage, than? A'll pent a sign
tae stick tae bins athort the toun
whit reads: *Miners' Club*. A haurd
o a faur-kent sculptor wha can spy
the angel in a block o stane,
n then o raggit fowk whit biggit
ceeties o raggit schuils amang
the shivers on his warkshap fluir.
A haurd o a public pailace (white tiles,
reid stane, oam thick wi steamin wirds)
prescrivit as rot n rubble by lanesome
scrans o men, n then o fowk
whit like tae gaither doots n dicht
n mend till aw the orras are glentin,
the doors are appen, n in the auld
is new is auld is auld is new.

The Hairdest Man in Govanhill

The hairdest man in Govanhill has thay lang white scairs on
  baith sides o his mooth fae smilin that damn wide.
        He tint twa teeth fae brushin ower sterly
        n his lips are gelt fae kissin babbies.
        His vyce shifts bus routes.

The hairdest man in Govanhill has airms like rebar fae
  cartin aboot auld folks' messages.
        He spits that haird hit colfs potholes.
        He pisses that haird hit dichts stairwalls
           blast-cleans
               n hit smells o roses n aw.
        He fairts that haird hit blaws the cloods fae the lift
        n the sun skyres haird on Victoria Street.

The hairdest man in Govanhill had tae stap playin fitba
  acause whanivver he fungt the baw hit brust
        but he'll staund in fer a missin goal post
        ithoot ye e'en askin.

The hairdest man in Govanhill can gar Cooncillors tae tell
  the truith
        juist by turnin his een in thair airtin
          fae up tae eleiven miles awa.

The hairdest man in Govanhill is that haird that whiles
  whan he reads the news
        sittin in his airmchair in the mids o the junction
        he juist
           greets
               pal, juist
                 greets

n the puils o his tears stap traffic
n weans sweem in thaim
n he greets hairder juist tae please thaim
   or mebbe at the sheer existence o thair
   lauchter in this warld
     oi
       aye
         this warld.

His chin is that haird he skives wi a risp n has a contract wi
 Brillo fer the clippins.
His feet are that haird Sustrans fee him tae fletten oot bike
 paiths wharivver thay fancy.
His nose is that haird hit cheesels the names o the deid on a
 hunner-year-auld heidstane.
His hair is that haird he gies hit tae canal-boats fer sweeng
 raips.
He's that bluidy haird he's a hairt tattooed wi Dulux on his
 bicep n aw hit says is *A LUV YE*.

When the hairdest man in Govanhill staps up tae ye n
 luiks ye haird in the ee n says in dymont soonds – *A'm the
 hairdest man in Govanhill* – he means
  Aye.
    Youse n aw.

Strong Female Character

She steps into shot in a flutey haze – hard lip,
soft focus, leaves and sunlight so, khakis both

practical and tight-fitting – for the demographic
of white teeth, hip-slung crossbows and tough

quips every other line. Strung up by script ink
in half-hearted half-formed fantasy, tossed off

between Dungeon Master and mistress. Tick, tick,
dev spec cinched. But pilot night, panicking staff

– glitch, glitch, screens flicker, static, clicks,
the SFX dept. clueless, the budget for 3D stuffed –

and here she stands before flatscreen and laptop. Blink.
She's larger than, well. She smiles. Someone coughs.

The carnage is Tarantino, or maybe Whedonesque.
The soundtrack grindcore for gothic bloodbath –

executives spiked; producers shafted on boom mics;
editors cut, cut, cut; all leading men pitched off the roof.

You get the picture. She gives the grin, the lick,
the hair-flick. Dollying shot, pull-back. Enough.

Alternate Ending

You get the picture. She gives the grin, the lick,
the hair-flick. Dollying shot, pull-back. She buffs

the gore from the blade-edge, reaches up and sticks
her knife through the paper ceiling, climbs up and off

the page. She takes another breath. She cracks her neck,
her lines, her author's back, and still it's not enough.

Bad Girls

you were always gonna be
the bad one / man how
does being the counterweight feel /
check / your plot was workshopped
well before you were born

don't play with dolls eliza /
you'll only get wet / you'll
only bite someone's heart out /
hell do what you want /
you do it so well

take me dancing and let's
vote you in / steer me
round the curves / no big
should you blow me up
or lick your pretty knife

you don't need to tell
your troubles / they're only vague /
straight out the special edition
figurine box / tell me you
don't get off on this

even reformed you won't even /
no daddy sub could learn
you with that lipstick / so
if you're not enjoying yourself
then you're doing something wrong

Showtime
a young lady's guide to vanquishing the undead

1. You will need an arena. Take into account lighting, inventory, sightlines, and opportunities for growth.

2. Your purpose is not to gut the monster but to gut the idea of the monster. Dress accordingly.

3. Wrap your weak points in adhesive strips: wrists, ankles, sternum. A taut neck is a valuable asset.

4. Acquire underlings with pliable skin.

5. When the session begins, recall the mission statement you wrote during training. If required, insert a long nail into your back for support.

6. The proper redrafting of strategic objectives is never a wasted hour: it means you will not need to land a blow. Pullback and recoil suffice. You are not a bird. You are not water.

7. Become the *I* in *leader*. Select weapons too heavy for illusion or grace. Become the piano-wire around the throat of the world.

8. Just watch.

9. Allocate tears as appropriate.

10. As you dust off, remember to factor the cost of the cleaning bill.

Your Strengths

Are you thrilled by excellence?
Are you always curious about the world?
Are you thrilled when you learn something new?
Can you bend to touch your knees and straighten up again?
Are most of your friends more imaginative than you?
What is the Enlightenment?
Can you use a pen or pencil?
Can you undo blouse buttons?
Can you recognise a friend?
Where does Father Christmas come from?

Can you walk 100 metres without repeatedly stopping?
Can you walk 50 metres without repeatedly stopping?
Can you walk at all?
Is walking good for the environment?
Do you avoid activities that are physically dangerous?
Do you make poor choices in friendships and relationships?
Do you change the subject when people pay you
    compliments?
Who defeated the Vikings?

Can you put on a hat?
Can you turn on a tap?
Who is the patron saint of Scotland?
Can you pick a light object off the floor?
If a police officer asks you to come to the station, do you
    have to go?
Can you put your arms behind your back?
Can you sit in a chair without needing to move?
What is it very important to do when engaging a solicitor?
Can you empty the catheter bag?

Do you have trouble accepting love from others?
Can your speech be understood by strangers?
Are you any good at planning group activities?
Are you able to fit in, no matter what the social situation?
Do you ever say funny things?
Do you mope a lot?

Do pain and disappointment often get the better of you?
Do you have control over the voiding of the bladder?
Does your life have a strong purpose?
Do you have a calling in life?
Who is the heir to the throne?

Do you lose concentration on a daily basis?
Do you lose control of bowels at least once a month?
What must all dogs wear in public?
Can you cope with minor changes to routine?
Can you complete a simple task?
Can you successfully complete a simple, everyday task?
Can you complete normal activities without overwhelming
    fear or anxiety?
Can you sustain any personal action?

Do you always say thank you, even for little things?
Do you stop and count your blessings?
Do you look on bright side?
Are you aware of the impact of your own behaviour?
What should you do if you spill someone's pint in the pub?
Are you any good at sensing what others are feeling?
Do you have a completely disproportionate reaction to
    criticism?
Do you have unpredictable outbursts of aggressive, bizarre
    behaviour?
Do you cause distress to others on a daily basis?
Can you pick up a pound coin?

Is the police force a public service that helps and protects?
What are the fundamental principles of British life?
Do you like to think of new ways to do things?
Is it a criminal offence to carry a weapon of any kind?
Are you able to look at things and see the big picture?
Do you need verbal instruction?
Do you have a well thought out plan for what you want to do?
How many pence are in the pound?
Can you see at all?
Can you let bygones be bygones?
Do you always try to get even?
Do you always finish what you start?

Sermon

Today, I want to focus my remarks on love.
Though the subject is complex, my message on love
is stark. We won't defeat love simply
by the actions we take outside our borders.

We have to get to the root of the problem.
We need to be clear on where the origins of love
lie. And we should be clear what we mean
by this term. It is a political ideology

supported by minorities. There are those
who use love to promote their goal. This is wrong.
We should cut ourselves off from love.
We have allowed the weakening of our collective identity.

All this leaves some lovers feeling rootless.
We see a process of radicalisation.
Internet chatrooms where attitudes are shared
and validated. In our communities,

groups led by young, dynamic lovers
define themselves solely in terms of their love.
These interactions are a substitute for what
wider society has failed to supply.

We must make it impossible
for lovers to succeed. We need to argue
that love is wrong. To belong here
is to believe in these things.

None of this will be easy. And it won't happen
if we act alone. This ideology
crosses continents. We are all
in this together. At stake is our way of life.

Supercut

We found my brother frozen at the position of the bodies all in deathly elegant hands with a single sure stroke can't hurt you and the faint smell of corruption was taken quickly in the bloody waters of the pleading for mercy as a golden sword had died birthing my brother by order of the rose petals spilling from her crushing blow from the fire in his gut was murdered in single combat on one another's swords had killed the hostages of meat and thick black sun was only a dozen from backbone to belly with the corpses to reconcile them beneath her bed and dashed his head against a king's throat in his own blood had burned that body to the stew before the beast wrenched back a rasher of her husband through the armour from the river and his three older brothers covered in dried litter, the prettiest, the most gentle and afterwards he had taken the one that crushed the life of his skull almost in two, and afterwards the king had said not a sudden death while his life's blood dried on a gilded head from the queen before her time died birthing a summer chill to the war when the walls had married and moved away and sometimes she confused suckling pig and pigeon was a great sadness for all at peace after the last of the pork pie in the hot blood inside the deer before a woman's head was chunks of brown meat cut down under the gorget with such force that it disgraced himself by killing six monstrous huge sweetbreads and pigeon pie and venison and fed her the first sweet body in the back of the skull before putting her to the sword who had died young and the hunting accident that had to be put down was dead before you could talk to his horse across the naked face of a whirlwind from the throat of a man in the shadowskin cloak as the animal screamed and buried the axe in the man's skull and left him cut down from behind while he stumbled over flesh and bone like rotten wood behind him and opened only the corpses of the thin, ragged men when found on the ground only three roast quail right out of a dozen good men had died to bring her skewers of charred meat and babes in red cloaks who gave a sickening horse in the rain running down his belly a red rain flying from a haunch of goat and a basket is dead slung across the back and a spray of bright white water turned red where the screaming man slid glistening blue snakes suddenly exploded out of the hand with the rest of the blow into his black heart and all her children shuddered and lay still in a crust of garlic and yanked back the man's head was turning above the flames, spitting and hissing and part of the the rest are stumbling and screaming till my mother burnt them all alive and those other poor women and children like dogs not a league from where we died for what remained of a blessed relief wrapped in the crimson sea you slew raw and bloody like nothing human through his eye is gone with a single sharp throat from shoulder to breastbone and leather and flesh by the time soaked red had killed with scarlet flowers were more across his eyes when she took it out and the steps were slick with roast chicken and she saw a body impaled with blue, blue eyes twisted completely around where they buried the carcass of a great white lion was slain and most of our men covered with ravens who profaned his blade so they might never reveal by a pig of the gods who won't be reporting back and we should have enough to bake the crows where he slew two of them to reveal the gleam of bone before it had buried it in his bowels when they cut down even the little fields of the dead and put an arrow through his behind to bleed and then a pile of corpses went tumbling through his throat filled the narrow, twisty lanes taller than he was, seared and crackling, a different fruit stabbed and opened, spiced and savoury, suspended over a roaring fire, skewered on the bones, his belly rumbling through their chests with his last red breath in full stride impaled on a man's ribs or finding flesh and leather and muscle and lungs and raked his blade with a sweeping downcut that entered his belly and buried his axe in a shower of blood and viscera lay in his lap had no mark but for the red bodies of the dead sword and split and dashed his head and the horse screamed and fountained as the young face seemed almost to explode for water between his eyes to pierce until she felt the bone atop the high red sighing sound, as if a million people had let out their breath at once who was beheaded so they faced out over the city and the birds had eaten one ear and he did not live when they were done with her and in the street I saw the cushion down across his face to wake a few more very gallant men and ripped apart a dozen still dead whenever the night wind gusted the spray of blood on the salt beef as well, and a rasher of bacon.

This is a customer security announcement

We apologise for the inconvenience.
For any inconvenience this may have caused.
We don't do these kinds of things.
You shouldn't be out to entrap people.
There was a piece of paper on the floor.
Our feet did come together. Apparently
they did bump. We won't dispute that.
We were doing research. It was followed
by a flood. We stood and waited. We go
to that bathroom regularly. We don't recall.
We don't recall taking this picture. We were
just giving him a ride home. We were just
playing along. The buffet car is now closed.
We've had surgery. He didn't stop breathing
or anything. We can't lift luggage.
That's why. We apologise for the delay.
Please allow the doors to close.
There has been an incident
on the crossing. We don't know.
That's not for us to decide.

Personal

Let's help each other out.
I'm in shape and I
have been fantasising
of being.

I'm seeking fashion forward
someone who makes her life
friendly to all occasions.
You feel happy and content.

It's time we meet.
I am very oriented.
I can get to know
and then who knows.

Here Be

In ten years time you will adopt a dragon. Maybe
from a shelter for unwanted cryptids, or just because
she landed in your back garden looking gorgeous but
a little sad about the nostrils. Either way,

you'll place a dish of charcoal on the kitchen floor
and immediately fall in love with her ankle-spurs,
her eyelashes (softer than the undragoned imagine),
the way she could roast you if she wanted, and might.

You will quickly get used to the smell of singed curtains.
You will move to a top-floor flat so she can practise
dead-drops down the stairwell. You will sing with her,
a tuneless, raucous clatter of song that'd send sleepless

neighbours into fury if it weren't so holy.
You will be astonished at the speed your life changes,
at how much time she has eaten, clockwork and all.
It's more than can be explained by her hot

scales through your jodpuhrs. Her wings are impossible,
the aerial views in her gift are impossible. She is
impossible. In eleven years time, you will finger the scar
on your cheek and hope that when she left you –

in flight or through a slit in air's fabric –
she meant to leave you with such a hoard of gold.

The action of descending rapidly from a height once the decision to land has been made

If we could fly – if arms were aerofoils
with cambered hands; if a brief jog
built airflow, lift; if up-stroke, down
-stroke, angle of attack were as natural
and hard-won as walking –

if all this, then most of us would
still drive. Internal combustion:
more relaxing than all that flapping.
The work of sparkplug, piston, oil.
Besides, air traffic control? Bloody

nightmare. There'd have to be
brightly-coloured fly-to-work schemes.
Vouchers for kids on cereal boxes.
Maps of scenic flight-plans, produced
by flushed-faced Greens. Proficiency tests.

Enthusiasts would invest in the right
helmets, arm-beacons, lycra, sure.
You'd always mean to get some
exercise, but couldn't bear the thought
of showing up sweat-patched.

In tourist-towns, rickshaw-flyers
with gorgeous deltoids would haul you home
from Friday night, so you could feel
the wind in your hair without all the hassle.
You'd look down. Look! those lights.

And the people. Wee dots. The ground.

Alpe d'Huez

It's the col of modernity. From the first edition, shown on live television, the Alpe d'Huez definitively transformed the way the Grande Boucle ran. No other stage has had such drama. With its 21 bends, its gradient and the number of spectators, it is a climb in the style of Hollywood.

– Jacques Augendre

rip
the mountain
down
the rippling vinyl mountain
down
tumble down

pearlescent
pearl
elbow thrown
petrol bouqet of glass and paint
splayed
turn up the bodies
our gold text splash
our switchback witch
piston limb success
yes be our
appalling
our
oh christ be our yellow streak
and sings
the shield wall
against
stains
the silver knuckle open fist of crowd
on the braggart odeon mountain

Saadiyat

a. INITIAL BASELINE

most buoyant property distraction marketing

    of people having fun and children playing in the clean

    brightly cut sails cut through the sparkling waters

      this is true island lifestyle

b. PRELIMINARY ECONOMIC IMPACT ANALYSIS

this multifunction facility its flow of visitors
and audiences the expertise and services of
two distinguished firms the vision was to
establish the real wealth of a country is not
it is its people we draw pride and the trees it
is   our   firm   reality
the significant corresponding expansion
and the development increase capacity
a   country   is   not
measured it is truly measured every person
no matter what we all need to know to
understand each other better gradually
developing into a growing organism this
arrangement interrupts the block matrix
exclusively reserved for privileged visitors

c. MASTER PLAN

His outstanding efforts
His humanitarianism
His beliefs
His vision
       a contemplative space
He recognised
He initiated
He understood
       the everyday existence
He knew that oil was
His answer was
He is a leader
       of the unifying symbols
His achievements
His visionary leadership
His actions
       the love and respect of the people
       their voices and memories
       the majesty of birds

d. SUSTAINABILITY

a core value integrated into the design approach
in terms of throughout the the the concept design and
detail stages and placed at the fore by going forward

    striving to reduce
        the impact
        the cultural context
        sensitivity
        the existing natural resources
            with a view to

    rationalising open space
    fostering greener living
    covered parking
        in appropriate areas

    where turtles nest and
    dolphins play in the surf
    hatching safely on
        Happiness Beach

e. OUTLOOK

                    water swirls
            sand banks stretch out
                    into the gulf

investment is encouraged
a tax-free environment
now open for viewing
the possibility which fills
the void left

                the rectangular grid
                    pattern loosens
                  curving informally

to lose your you
you become you must become
the real silence is to
approach this silence you
do not go and then

                determining the potential
                  estimating the annual
                approximating the capital

under construction
under construction
u/c
u/c
u/c

f. MONEY-BACK GUARANTEE

If you are not satisfied with
either the product or the purchase
price, you may return the product
in original packaging and with
undamaged sealing without
reasons. Within ten days after
purchase. Please also include
your bank details. We will refund
the purchase price plus/minus
the amount equivalent to
the percentage change.

You Don't Ever Have To Lose

a. OUR SONG

The Atos automated cyclamen ordering telegram is simple, secure and reliable. Our busybody telecommunications will tale a song to meet your specific commissioned obscenities and technical researchers.

We will reflect and communicate your brat! Our speckled tear-jerker will enthrone the utopian interloper and the upholders themselves will fixate on your distinctive epic.

Getting started with automated ordering telegrams could not be easier: once we've agreed a technical spectre with you, we can despair and install a pinch-song within twelve weigh-ins. From there it is but a simple proclamation to scan up to a full song.

b. SUN NUMBER

Changed flow and connected income leaked sunny
away too long your eyes only so to bed

I was a boy from hell beneath your beautiful London eye
factors systems numbers workers the wild management

Problems for you, guy with the glasses, solving storm
blood complaints sun perfume value

In music the land for a star to fall in love with
sun   centre   shop   life   trade   shop

Were the days you let the sun in there to order time?
distance   service   time   service   lyrics

c. BENEFITS

Terms and auto service technology.
The industry is constant.
Automatic alignment of the proposed method.
Simple and immediate benefits to customers.
Rest, because they were in the past.

Geotdoyi! *wait for the series resistance*

Pubs, bars, restaurants, and more benefits.
Optimum performance and maximum time.
Effective to sell. Easy to touch.
So you can attract more.
Customers and revenue.

Geotdoyi! *wait for the series resistance*

You manage and execute.
Daily specials are based on real time.
The most important is that consumers they were.
Provide excellent security solutions too.
Availability and reliability.

Geotdoyi! *wait for the series resistance*

Our self-monitoring system was.
Productivity and likes and dislikes and.
Understand promotion can really.
Customer requirements and.
Depending on the market.

Geotdoyi! *wait for the series resistance*

Tae a Cooncillor
on his clossin anither sweemin puil wi his cuts

Wee glaikit, skybald, fashious bastart,
whit unco warld maks ye wir maister?
Whit glamour has ye risin fest as
      projectile boak?
Hit's time tae gie yer feechie fouster
      an honest soak.

Hit's fowk like ye will aye tak pouer,
houivver smaw, tae reassure
yer scrinkit sowel ye arenae puir
      like aw aroond ye;
n when yer perk is quite secuir
      thair wrath astoonds ye.

Sae ye bou yer pus tae gods like profit
the mair tae rax the troch n scoff it,
the mair tae mooth the needfu: *Tough! It's
      a striver's Scotland.*
A'm here tae learn ye nou, come off it,
      yer patter's rotten.

Ye an aw the fowk wha's like ye:
schuilyaird bangster wi mankit psyche,
polis runnin a schemie reich wi
      Protect n Sairve,
mid-heid-bummer wha sneists a spiky
      Mair'n ma joab's warth.

A'd hink that rogues wad hae ambition,
wad aim fer a CEO's position,
wad be PM-type politicians,
        the mair tae plunder;
but ye're content wi shilpit visions
        n skirvin wonder.

A ken that we shuid haud oor laith
fer duimsters whit are warth oor braith;
but maugre o yer mickle stouth
        ye're muckle gruesome:
ye'll cut the leebries, cut the baths,
        cut aw whit's luesome,

cut aw whit fowk hae cam tae treisur.
Yer life's sae tuim yer anely pleisur
is crousely usin rule n meisur
        tae cut whit vieve
ye cannae unnerstaund, whit leisur
        we need tae live.

(A'll tak a spell afore concludin
Tae say ma flytin's no includin
the fowk in Cooncils no colludin
        in yer fustian rule,
who tak thair pouer n spreid it, pruivin
        thay'd jyne the puil.)

Sae ken ye nou, wir teen's expandin;
we'll pind whit's oors n, nowithstandin
the wheen wha's leal, we'll lauch, disbandin
        yer pack n aw,
n tho no first, ye will be standin
        against the waw.

Shoud ma wirds seem awfie sterie,
a weird whit's oot o whack, a theory
owergane – yer wrangs war peerie –
        A'll wiss insteid
Ye see yersel as ithers see ye:
        awready deid.

Ye've wan chaunce still tae reest yer ghaist –
yer seilie fer that's mair than maist
will get fae ye – sae mak yer cast,
        A'm yet gey steamin.
Nou, Cooncillor, resign yer post
        n get tae sweemin.

Hogmanay

Let's be arsonists. Let's birn the year.
Let's kirsten ilka month in ile n pit a lunt
tae day wan. Hit wis that guid. Let's mak like airtists
n birn the leebrars acause we shoudna, n birn
Pairlament acause we shoud. Let's big a bale
o awhing whit's bonnie n awhing whit isna
n birn it. Och it'll be grand. The kittlins will birn.
The bunnet firs will birn. The traffeck will birn.
The foggie-bees will birn. The oceans will birn. Aye the fires
will bluim like birses on the yird, whit'll birn,
n the sun will birn, n the planets o gas will birn,
n the planets o frost will birn, n whan the universe
haes catcht n wants nae mair tenderness fae us,
we will birn oorsels, n the thocht o fire.

Neither can we call this a begging of misery

a cyclist tricks the keys in her pocket / a line-cook
trills spittle over the locally-sourced / a chicken plucks
herself from the egg-groove / oooh it is murder / the squawk /
the curtain / the quietus / an engine glosses herself in a blank
cheque of scorch and smoke / a park heaves her hummocks /
ejects sixty-six cops / one bank / eight roadblocks /
makes a fist of each fountain / a three-year-old packs
up the alphabet / chucks the toys out / sticks
her tongue in the hi-tech crib's socket / spies a godly spark
and shoves up two infant digits / a grimace / a clerk
prefers not to / here / here / here / here / I urge you take
these knives to heart / suck failure to a pink and vicious spike /
make loss your hearth now / here kindling / a hunk
of frank admiration / here luck / here hold / our reeking book

Scenes fae a Protest

auld wifie brang a poly bag
luikit pangit wi sandwiches
A thocht ye'd need this
sheu'd spent oors makkin thaim
watter bombs

*

we haed walkie-talkies
the fowk inside wad say
eh eh eh
coud ye get us
a packit o twinty fags?

*

we got the caw
that thay were comin
ran doun
linkit airms
rashin wi rain

*

ma young boy wis
on the front page
o the mornin edition
by the evenin edition
he wis replaced by horses

*

whit thay cried a riot
let's cry hit a rammie aye
let's cry hit that / hit wis
sair fit but
some fun but

*

bluidy pineapple! whar
wad we get a pineapple?
naw thair wis mebbe
five hunner eggs but I nivver
saw a pineapple

*

wee man sportit a helmet
maircht the station
n luved hit / A dinna
hink the polis
were that impressed

*

hit wis aw very
at the end A mean
hit wis aw very
tragic tho
here we are nou

Aald rede fir biggin a kintra

versions after the Tao Te Ching, September 2014

20

nae laernan, nae deul

atween YES an NO
        whit odds?
atween geud an ill
        whit odds?
dreid whit aabody dreids?
        – glintid!

fock gangan
as fir a belly-rive
but a'm tawie, wirdless
as a bairn at's nivver smiled
forfaren, ithoot a haem tae mesel

aabody's fouthie
        an a'm alone
a geup mynd
        steero, steero

aabody's gleg
        an a'm driftan
i the tide
        laar-snuvid

aabody's ettlan
        an a'm thraan
alone, unkan
        bab i the creel

29

ettlan tae ower the warld?
    nae chance

the warld's a cog o spirit
    an canno be owered

wha owers, fails
wha haads, tints

        some laed, some follae
        some greet, some lilt
        some rapple, some cryne
        some thirl, some brak

syne the aald i the horn
    fire oot waste an wanthrift

36

tae hint, skael
tae sap, brace
tae ban, big
tae end, faa til

      caa this a subtle laem

saft an swack wins stark an stieve
fish canno jouk the weel
      a kintra's best wappens
      canno be kythed

53

a bit wittins
whan waakan the wey
        are a rod tae dree

the wey is snod
an fock cheust fancy the ramse

govrenment divided
        sheens growen-up
        kists empie
but heidyins' claes are braa
        thay've barrie blads
        are stecht wi maet
        gey rowthie

caa this the darg o reivers
        an no the wey

57

the mair the laas
      the peurer the fock
the sneller the blads
      the mair the strowe
the sleer the sleyts
      the waar the wark
the mair the ring
      the mair the crime

syne

      dinno deu
n fock transform thirsels
      mak still
n fock govren thirsels
      growe teum
n fock growe fouth
      want no
n fock growe haemelt

61

a muckle kintra
      lowdens hidsel
an baets a peedie wan

a peedie kintra
      bides lowden
an baets a muckle wan

      whiles lowdenan baets
      whiles bidan lowden baets

a muckle kintra wants
      tae haen fock
a peedie kintra wants
      tae ser fock

      fir baeth tae win
      the muckle wan maan lowden

80

peedie kintra, curn o fock
       haep o gibbles
       nivver haaden

fock mynd on deith
       an dinna fare far
thay've whirls an yoles
       at neebdy hurls
guns n graith
       at neebdy wags
thay coont wi raes an raep

       hinnie leevin
       bonnie claes
       lown haems
       lillie dances

neebor kintras bide that closs
       ye'll hear thir baests
but bairns growe aald an dee
       no needan tae cam an gang

Gloamin
version after Abdel Rahim al-Sheikh

thare's a bird, alane   alane n mettin the may sun wi the dirl o his weengs,
mair aiver as the east, he preens, speeds by, sneds the ben heid, a feather hairp,
kent tae luvers by his blinkers, his fell fling, his acrobat towe-tap greenin, his twa black feet
n aw is fleetin but him, the camera shutter, the lip-fou rainbowe   warld ithoot end or dule
n he's no the nicht warden, disna tell ilka dawin o the nicht returnin at sundoun,
but the nicht will aye return, n the feather hairp   a luver oot o luck n a luck oot o luve,
a trystin place, a burn, an ingle, a lip o aw hings, again n again,
his feints n flits were far fae tender   he sattles on her breist, as roond as the warld,
haudin in his butterflees, a hap fer the murnin; his marrae in sowfin,
n his soufu dwaums merch on, n thare's nae chairts fer the crossin, n sheu warns him:
that bairn, yer watter, is takkin aff his buits, is leanin on the muntains o the muin,
a soond whar airts brak, a slockin blue, a mirkie pairl...

    aw his fire! aw his fluit!
    aw the shiftin warld!

    n wha maks the utmaist turn!

67

Further Drafts

work as if you live in the early days of a better nation
     shirk as if you live in the early days of a better vacation
smirk as if you live in the early days of a better notion
     perk as if you live in the early days of a better potion
jerk as if you live in the early days of a better lotion
     twerk as if you live in the early days of a better motion
irk as if you live in the early days of a better mission
     lurk as if you live in the early days of a better sedition

Notes

The Scots used throughout is mongrel and magpie, like the English. It mostly follows the Report an Recommends o the Scots Spellin Comatee, with a few personal variations ("n" for "an"/"and", "hit" for "it", "hing" for "thing"). *Aald rede fer biggin a kintra* is in Orcadian rather than Scots, with a different but related grammar, orthography and vocabulary. www.dsl.ac.uk will translate both Scots and Orcadian words, and English glosses of all the Scots poems are available at www.harrygiles.org/englishglosses.

In *Song for a Lover as Magicicada*, the magicicada septendecim (or Pharaoh cicada), of which Brood X is the largest brood, is singing *Pharaoh* as sung by Sidney Carter and recorded by Alan Lomax. *If you measure the distance...* refers to a study of Jurassic cricket fossils as recorded in the Proceedings of the National Academy of Sciences vol. 109 no. 10. *Bad Girls* and *Showtime* are written for *Buffy the Vampire Slayer* S03E14 and S07E11 respectively.

Slash poem in which... is made from extracts from Harry Styles fanfiction. *Your Strengths* is made entirely from questions in the Department for Work and Pensions Work Capability Assessment, the Life in the UK Citizenship Test, and the DWP's bogus *Your Strengths* psychometric test. *Sermon* is an adaptation of a speech given by David Cameron to the Munich Security Conference. *Supercut* samples every mention of death in George R R Martin's *A Game of Thrones. This is a customer security announcement* quotes male homophobic-voting American politicians exposed in sexual encounters with men. *Personal* quotes online personals ads. *Saadiyat* is an artificial island and cultural centre in Abu Dhabi; the poem is made from texts in an industrial exhibition about its construction. *You Don't Ever Have To Lose* applies chance operations to an advertising sheet from IT services company Atos.